MAN'S
INHUMANITIES

HUMAN TRAFFICKING

By Thom Winckelmann

ERICKSON PRESS
Yankton, South Dakota

© 2009 Erickson Press

Printed in the United States of America

For more information, contact:
Erickson Press
329 Broadway
PO Box 33
Yankton, SD 57078

Or you can visit our Web site at **www.ericksonpress.com**

Content Consultant:
Professor Mark Bernstein
Joyce and Edward E. Brewer Chair in Applied Ethics
Philosophy Department, Purdue University

Editor: Amy Van Zee
Copy Editor: Paula Lewis
Design and Production: Becky Daum

Library of Congress Cataloging-in-Publication Data
Winckelmann, Thom.
  Human trafficking / by Thom Winckelmann.
     p. cm. — (Man's inhumanities)
  Includes bibliographical references (p.) and index.
  ISBN 978-1-60217-978-3 (alk. paper)
1. Human trafficking. 2. Slave trade. I. Title. II. Series.

  HQ281.W56 2009
  306.3′62--dc22

                                    2008034806

CONTENTS

MODERN-DAY SLAVES

When you hear the term *human trafficking*, what do you think of? In the United States, the earliest example of human trafficking might have been the slave trade. Millions of slaves were brought to the Americas from Africa. This began in the 1600s. It continued to the mid-1800s. This slave trade included Africa, the Americas, and Europe. It displaced millions of people. But we are wrong to assume that human trafficking is a thing of the past.

If you were to open a newspaper and see a headline about human trafficking, would you be surprised? Human trafficking is a very current issue. In the early 1800s, the United States passed legislation banning the slave trade. But human beings are still being transported for wrong and often illegal purposes.

The African slave trade might be what most of us think of when we hear the term *human trafficking*.

President George W. Bush held a news conference in 2004. The conference took place in Tampa, Florida. His speech highlighted the importance of the issue. But the president's remarks did not deal with old news. He was not talking about slaves of the past. He was talking about people who were currently living in slavery. He also spoke about what the United States must do to end slavery once and for all.

President Bush spoke at the National Conference on Human Trafficking in 2004.

The president spoke about human trafficking. He talked about the trade of human beings. Just like the early slave traders, people continue to enslave other human beings. They transport others within nations, across borders, and over the seas. They take them to places where they will live and work in slavery. Some people are enslaved until they can repay a debt. Others are enslaved until they escape or die. However, none live in freedom. And none enjoy the basic human rights we take for granted.

Chapter 1

WHAT IS HUMAN TRAFFICKING?

When we hear the term *traffic*, most of us think of cars moving along a road. But the term *trafficking* also means "to deal or trade in something illegal." We might hear news stories of the police charging a person with trafficking in stolen merchandise. In rare instances, we might even hear the phrase *human trafficking*. This is the illegal transport and trade of human beings.

Why not use the term smuggling instead? Smuggling may involve merchandise that is legal. Smuggling means that something is transported illegally. For example, merchandise might be smuggled to avoid the payment of taxes. In the case of human smuggling, it may describe the transport of people with their permission. People who help others who want to cross a national border without the required documents are smugglers. They are not

These people are from Brazil. They were trying to enter the United States illegally.

human traffickers. Victims of human trafficking do not give their consent.

Human trafficking is described as modern-day slavery. In terms of human rights, human trafficking is a major world issue. In 2008, a New York man and his wife were convicted for keeping household workers in slave-like conditions. The man, Mahender Sabhnani, was sentenced to three and a half years in prison. His wife Varsha, however, received a much longer sentence. The victims were Indonesian women. Varsha confiscated their passports. According to the victims, they often worked 20-hour days and were not fed properly. They were punished by being forced to walk up and down stairs repeatedly. They had boiling water poured on them. Varsha was sentenced to 11 years in prison for her mistreatment of the domestic workers. The prosecutors estimated that Varsha and her husband owed the workers more than $1 million in compensation for their work. The case brought the issue of modern slavery to light. Slavery is still occurring within U.S. borders.

During the pre-Civil War era in the African slave trade, slaves were captured by force. It is hard to imagine people being captured and enslaved today as they were at that time. In many cases they are not.

Domestic Slave

A woman named Supik Indrawati is one example of an illegal slave worker. She came from Indonesia to work for a U.S. businessman. She was forced to work in his home. "Working from an English-Indonesian dictionary and a children's library book, Indrawati managed to pencil a letter to the police: 'dear mr police office sir,' she laboriously wrote. 'please please please I really need your help police officer sir. . . .'"[1]

Eight countries added to human traffic list

The State Department added eight countries, including four U.S. allies, to its list of nations with poor performance in combatting human trafficking. The Victims Protection Act of 2002 requires the department to report annually to Congress with an assessment of human trafficking in the world.

U.S. State Department report on human trafficking, 2005

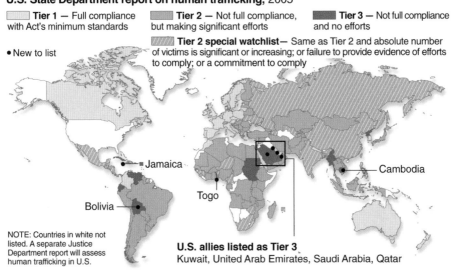

Tier 1 — Full compliance with Act's minimum standards

Tier 2 — Not full compliance, but making significant efforts

Tier 3 — Not full compliance and no efforts

Tier 2 special watchlist — Same as Tier 2 and absolute number of victims is significant or increasing; or failure to provide evidence of efforts to comply; or a commitment to comply

• New to list

Jamaica

Cambodia

Togo

Bolivia

NOTE: Countries in white not listed. A separate Justice Department report will assess human trafficking in U.S.

U.S. allies listed as Tier 3
Kuwait, United Arab Emirates, Saudi Arabia, Qatar

SOURCE: State Department

AP

The United States is a leader in actively working to fight human trafficking.

However, many victims of human trafficking may suffer from both force and coercion. To coerce means to cause people to do something by persuading them or forcing them. For example, traffickers may use violence at first. Afterward, they may only have to threaten to use violence again. By using force, they can get their victims to do what they want them to do. Coercion may also involve threats against a family member or loved one. Victims are less likely to try to resist, escape, or alert the police if they believe their families may be harmed. Traffickers may also coerce their victims by separating them and then threatening them with harm. Traffickers do this to friends, siblings, parents and children, or husbands and wives. Once apart, the victims are made to fear that they must obey or their loved ones will suffer. The people they believe they are protecting are often subject to the same threats.

Although slavery still occurs, it is difficult to imagine a ship full of enslaved people arriving on U.S.

These Chinese workers were rescued from their slave labor. They worked in brick kilns.

shores today. How do traffickers move their victims from place to place without being caught? Ships and trucks transport human traffickers' victims across borders and within countries. However, many victims are moved in a way that is far less likely to result in their discovery. It is also less likely to result in the arrest of their traffickers. In such cases, victims transport themselves. Why would people allow themselves to become victimized? They do so only because another method commonly used by human traffickers is fraud. Fraud means using deceit or tricks to get someone to do something. It often involves people pretending to be something they are not.

In this age of technology and instant communications, it is easy for human traffickers to

An American Duty

"The American government has a particular duty, because human trafficking is an affront to the defining promise of our country. People come to America hoping for a better life. And it is a terrible tragedy when anyone comes here, only to be forced into a sweatshop, domestic servitude, pornography or prostitution."[2]

—George W. Bush, July 16, 2004

Human traffickers can lure victims using false advertisements on the Internet. This Ukrainian man was arrested for a large Internet fraud scam.

place false advertisements. They no longer have to risk going to a newspaper office or calling the telephone company. The Internet lets them place ads around the world. They may claim to be seeking tutors, restaurant staff, translators, or household employees. They do not use a telephone number that may be traced by the police.

EVERY MINUTE OF THE DAY...

A WOMAN OR A CHILD IS SOLD

The Movement Against Trafficking held a rally in India on January 12, 2008.

Instead, they may use an anonymous e-mail account. Unsuspecting victims are lured by the promise of a high-paying job. Sometimes they are promised the opportunity to travel. Only after arriving at their destination do they learn the truth.

Human traffickers do not always use anonymous methods to seek victims. Sometimes they use people to act as recruiters. These traffickers seek out victims of a certain age, gender, or physical appearance. In order to gain access to potential victims, recruiters may visit parks, shopping malls, nightclubs, or even schools. In one case, a teenage girl befriended other teens at her school. She told them that her father would hire them to do cleaning work. The father gained the trust of the victim. The victim was eventually drugged, raped, and beaten. Other traffickers target runaways and teens who are involved with drugs. In some cases, traffickers lure victims with the promise of a relationship or even marriage.

Teenagers are not the only people victimized by human traffickers. As many as 80 percent of trafficking victims are female. Half are children. According to a 2004 White House address, 400,000 to 600,000 people are trafficked each year. Fifty thousand such people enter the United States annually. They are trafficked to any country with a demand for agricultural laborers, domestic servants, prostitutes, or manufacturing workers. What they share in common is that they are victims. In all, it is estimated that nearly 30 million victims of human trafficking live and work in some form of slavery today.

Chapter 2

THE DEMAND FOR CHEAP LABOR

*W*hy is there still a demand for slaves? Today's business community is a vibrant one. The global economy has grown to an unimagined size. Technology is advancing and consumer demands are changing. These changes force business owners to be in touch with new trends. Their employees, equipment, products, and advertising messages all must be adaptable. If the company is to stay in business and remain competitive, the business must stay up to date. Business owners must continually reinvest a portion of their profits in education, training, and modernization.

Labor-intensive industries can be difficult and costly to modernize. If something is labor-intensive, it requires the work of many people to run smoothly. This type of work is often manual. These industries include agriculture, assembly, and some forms of

These workers labor to build leather bags in one of India's largest slums.

manufacturing. Other examples include restaurants and hotel businesses. Labor is one of the most significant costs in these types of businesses. This is among the reasons so many companies outsource parts of their operations. Outsourcing means that the companies send some of their work to workers outside the company. They outsource to countries where labor is less expensive than in the United States. Maintaining overseas facilities helps them keep their products competitively priced. It also helps them continue to earn a substantial profit.

Some argue that outsourcing is simply a way of delaying the modernization that must take place. People who oppose outsourcing believe that inexpensive labor is an excuse for businesses to avoid the expense of modernizing. Opponents of outsourcing use the outdated methods of plantation owners in the pre-Civil War southern United States as an example. Industries that make use of unpaid labor today have just as little incentive to change

Outsourcing is a way for American companies to utilize cheap labor. Many companies outsource to India. Some Indian companies overwork their employees, causing health problems such as sleep disorders and depression.

The Ethics of Slavery

According to the BBC, everyone agrees that slavery is unethical. The news group estimates that despite that fact, there are more victims of slavery today than there were during the Atlantic slave trade. Why does slavery persist? Poverty, debt bondage, and population growth are possible factors. Crime, corruption, and lack of law enforcement are other reasons.

as slave owners did then. As long as there are human traffickers to provide workers, some business owners can avoid the risks and expenses associated with operating a competitive business in today's modern, global economy.

Unlike the United States in the mid-nineteenth century, slavery is illegal almost everywhere today. Even though it is illegal, it is still happening. Modern-day slave owners and the people who traffic in human beings have further incentive. It is far cheaper to buy a slave today than it was for plantation owners in the South before the Civil War. This takes into account inflation and the cost of living. At one time, slave ownership required an investment that would be equal to several thousand dollars today. But by contrast, an enslaved male can be purchased in the Ivory Coast (Cote d'Ivoire) today for as little as $35. Girls might be bought in western Africa for $1,200 each. On the average, trafficked human beings might cost $500 or less. The profits they earn for their traffickers and those who take advantage of them as a source of unpaid labor are far greater.

It is tempting to compare human trafficking to the transport and sale of illegal drugs or weapons. Unlike these products, however, trafficked humans are a long-term venture. Joy Zarembka of the Campaign for Migrant Domestic Workers Rights puts it this way: "You can use them over and over and over again. You don't just sell them once and call it a day. It's very, very profitable."[1] The profits mean that the

Sold like Cabbages

A Thomson Reuters news article reported on children being sold in China. The children worked on farms. Some of the children were under ten years old. "Thousands of children in southwest China have been sold into slavery like 'cabbages,' to work as labourers in more prosperous areas such as the booming southern province of Guangdong."[2]

AUG 25 2003
5:34:38PM

A rebel force in Peru held these women and children as slave laborers and forced them to grow crops.

demand for this ongoing source of unpaid labor is widespread. It might be easier for us to think that human trafficking is something that occurs far outside of U.S. borders. But the truth is that trafficked humans are in places much closer to our homes. Human trafficking is a transnational business. This means that it occurs across national borders. Human trafficking provides laborers wherever there is a demand. This includes Western Europe and the United States, as well as Africa, the Middle East, Asia-Pacific, and Asia.

It is difficult to estimate the number of humans trafficked into the United States each year. But it is clear that there are tens of thousands of victims. Additional people fall prey to traffickers within U.S. borders. This only adds to the number of victims. Many of the trafficking victims in the United States work in agriculture. Many arrive after falling for a fraud. They might have been lured with the promise of a good-paying job. Many more have been smuggled into the country as undocumented immigrants.

Five women were held captive as sex slaves in this home in DeWitt, New York. This room is part of an underground bunker.

These child laborers were rescued in Bombay, India, in 2006. The police freed more than 250 children who were working in small-scale factories.

In this case, they most often would have been "helped" into the country in exchange for money. They are lured by the dreams of freedom and

Varsha Sabhnani was sentenced to 11 years in prison for abusing two Indonesian housekeepers. She kept them in near slavery in her Long Island, New York, mansion.

opportunity in the United States. These victims promise to pay far more than they can afford. Their traffickers offer to let them work to repay their debts. The traffickers then charge for food, lodging, and other expenses. Their goal is to make the victims' debt increase far more quickly than their savings. In effect, these victims become indentured servants. They are working in debt bondage to their captors. This means that the victims agree to work in order to pay off money that they owe to someone. But in most cases, they are never able to earn enough to pay off their debts and go free. They may work under the threat of violence to themselves or their families. Many are told that if they try to escape, the family in their home country will be harmed. In any case, they are kept isolated in a strange country. They have no documents. The victims lack the means to communicate with people who might help them.

Florida is one of the most popular vacation destinations in the United States. It is also among the most common places to find human trafficking victims. The state has a diverse economy and population. It also has a population of people who live there only for certain parts of the year. This population also includes many tourists. These elements combine to make

Cheap Labor Needs

"All you have to do is look where cheap labor is required and where there is a potential for labor exploitation, which pretty much can put you anywhere in our state."[3]

—Robin Thompson,
Florida Human Trafficking Researcher

unpaid workers in high demand. They are needed in a number of key industries that demand labor.

In the summer of 2005, vacationers were enjoying Florida's beaches and many attractions. But federal law enforcement officials were planning a raid on a farm in Palatka. Palatka is a small city in eastern Florida. Homeless men and women had been lured there by the promise of work, food, pay, and a place to live. Instead, they found themselves in debt bondage to the owners of a potato farm. They lived in primitive conditions. They did not have electricity or running water, despite the heat and difficult work they endured. The farm owners provided food and a place to live. They told the workers that they could work to pay off their living costs. The captors also had alcohol and drugs available. They did everything they could to make sure that the workers owed them more than

Sentencing

Maude Paulin received a sentence that was longer than those declared guilty in other similar cases. Prosecutor Edward Chung stated, "This is an extremely serious crime."[4] He remarked that her punishment was harsh so that others would not repeat her crime.

they could repay. At the time of the raid, more than 100 workers lived and labored in the confines of the camp. State, local, and federal authorities have found similar cases at farms, groves, hotels, and worksites around the state.

Domestic servants are also in demand. Human traffickers prey upon this need. Many people want one or more household staff to assist them with cleaning, laundry, and other chores. Some people hire undocumented workers. They do this so that they can offer low wages. Often, they can also avoid paying taxes. Others avoid paying wages altogether by using trafficking victims. A retired middle school teacher in Miami was arrested with her mother in 2007. They had agreed to sponsor a girl from Haiti to work for them in the United States. The girl was 16 years old. Once the girl arrived in Miami, they took her passport and other documents. For the next six years, she suffered verbal and physical abuse. She slept on the floor and was given little to eat. She worked as many as 15 hours each day. But she received no pay. She escaped when she was 22. Maude Paulin, her captor, was sentenced to prison for seven years. Her sentence was one year longer than she held the Haitian girl in captivity.

Chapter 3

SOLDIERS AND THE SEX TRADE

*B*oys and young men who become victims of human trafficking often work in man-ufacturing or agriculture. In some parts of the world, they are forced to become soldiers or to support military operations. In doing so, their lives are at risk. In other cases, they may be forced to give up their lives as suicide bombers. Traffickers also prey on girls and women. They force these women to spend months or years working as factory or farm laborers. Some become domestic servants. Others perform dangerous work in or near war zones. Many of the girls and women who are trafficked each year are selected specifically for their age and their appearance. Their captors intend to use them for profit in prostitution.

In one case, a girl from Pensacola, Florida, became the victim of trafficking. But the trafficking was not for agricultural or domestic work. It was for an entirely

Sex Trafficking

U.S. law gives the following definition to sex trafficking:

"Sex trafficking [is] a commercial sex act . . . induced by force, fraud, or coercion, or in which the person induced to perform such act has not attained 18 years of age."[1]

different purpose. The girl was a high school student named Shauna. She befriended a new girl at school. After a time, Shauna got to know the new girl's father as well. He was friendly to Shauna. She liked and trusted both of them. It turned out that Shauna's new friend and her father were human traffickers. The girl posed as the man's daughter. She was actually an adult. She was not related to him by blood. But she was his partner in crime. Her job was to "recruit" people at the local high school. She told Shauna she could earn money by working for her father. She claimed he operated a cleaning business. This caused Shauna to become comfortable with the idea of going out of town. She would be gone overnight with her new friend, her father, and with strangers. Shauna went over to her friend's house for what she thought would be a trip out of town. Instead, she was drugged, beaten, and raped. She was eventually able to escape after four days. But before she did, she overheard her captors talking about bringing her to another state. They were going to force her to work in prostitution. Many girls and women have similar stories. Not all are lucky enough to escape.

A police raid on a Bethesda, Maryland, brothel revealed shocking cases of slavery. A brothel is a house or building where prostitutes are available. In the late 1990s, authorities discovered that the women working there had been smuggled into the country illegally. Translators helped interview the women

Some brothels are hidden behind a legal business. Here, a massage parlor is a disguise for a brothel.

after the raid. The police realized that the women had been working there as slaves. The business owners had taken their identification and other documents. The women were coerced into working there against their will. They were beaten. They were threatened that there would be more violence. Many human trafficking victims come from countries that have or once had governments that controlled every aspect of the citizens' lives. In this case, these women did not realize that they could trust the authorities. They thought they were alone. They believed that no one could help them. They were enslaved until the police raid freed them. There was another similar police raid in Las Vegas. It revealed dozens of women being held

Prostitution is legal in some countries. However, leaders of these countries recognize that legalized prostitution does not help stop sex trafficking.

against their will. There are certainly other men, women, and children in the world who are being held captive in similar circumstances. But it is uncertain how long it will take to free all of these people from their captors.

Child Soldiers

Human Rights Watch is a nongovernmental organization. Human Rights Watch works on resolving issues such as genocide, torture, and slavery. The organization is a member of the fight against human trafficking. It lists nearly two dozen nations around the world that use trafficked children for horrifying purposes. These child slaves do not work in factories or fields. Most would consider themselves lucky to become domestic servants. Some of them—both boys and girls—do end up serving the sexual desires of their adult captors. But that is usually not their main function. Instead, these children carry rifles and rocket launchers for armies and militias. They fight in wars, rebellions, and uprisings.

Some of these child soldiers were kidnapped in raids upon their towns or villages. Others were taken as prisoners of war and forced to fight for their captors. Some lost their families to conflict and sought the safety of the armed forces. Then they found themselves

Under Our Noses

Kim Kennedy is a producer for the CBS *Early Show*. She commented on the sex trade and human trafficking: "For weeks I didn't actually believe the story I was working on. I thought it must be hype. Enslaving teenagers for prostitution could not be happening under our noses."[3]

forced onto the battlefield. Some of these children are as young as eight years old. Some are used as human mine detectors because they are too small and weak to carry weapons and ammunition. Even if they are big enough to fight, they lose their childhood and their innocence in the process. As many as 300,000 child trafficking victims are in armies and militias today.

The vast majority of these child soldiers are there against their will. Children at a young age can be easily

These children are soldiers in Zaire, Africa.

This young Burmese boy is a member of the Karen National Union (KNU). The KNU is a rebel group opposed to the ruling government.

persuaded. Many of these children are coerced into committing violent acts. They may think that the leaders of the armed forces will take care of them. They might trust their leaders. Through continued exposure to

Niger
Chad
Sudan
Eritrea
Dijbouti
Nigeria
Ethiopia
Central African Republic
Cameroon
Somalia
Equatorial Guinea
Uganda
Kenya
Gabon
Congo
Dem. Rep.
of Congo
Rwanda
Burundi
Tanzania
Angola
Malawi
Zambia
Mozambique
Zimbabwe
Namibia
Madagascar
Botswana

Reports show that children are used as soldiers by groups in Angola, Burundi, the Democratic Republic of Congo, Rwanda, Sudan, and Uganda in Africa.

violence, the children can become brainwashed. Most of these children are in Africa. Others are with militias, rebel groups, and terrorist organizations. These organizations are in Colombia, Sri Lanka, and the Middle East, for example. However, not all are forced to serve as soldiers. Some take on other roles.

Among the many dangers faced by U.S. and British troops in Iraq are children. In May 2008, the Associated Press reported that al-Qaeda had begun using children to serve as suicide bombers. The Associated Press had a source in the Iraqi government. The source said that the terrorist group's leaders believed children would be more likely to reach their targets without being stopped by security forces. One captured training video showed children

In the Democratic Republic of Congo in Africa, tribal fighting has killed hundreds of people. Armies from other countries have stepped in to stop the violence.

Threats of Violence

One of the boys who was forced to train as a suicide bomber talked with reporters. He said, "The Saudi insurgent threatened to rape our mothers and sisters, destroy our houses and kill our fathers if we did not cooperate with him."[4]

as young as ten years old being trained to build and detonate bombs.

A raid on an al-Qaeda site in the city of Mosul freed a group of boys who were being forced to undergo such training. They ranged in age from as young as 14 to 18 years old. They were brought to a nearby police station. Tearfully, they described what had happened to them. These children were rescued. No one knows for certain how many child soldiers around the world will be rescued.

Chapter 4

CHILD VICTIMS OF HUMAN TRAFFICKING

C hildren represent about half of the victims of human trafficking. As many as 15 million children live in some form of slavery today around the world. Most victims are from the Asia-Pacific region, Southeast Asia, Eastern Europe, Latin America, and Africa. As many as 10,000 to 15,000 children from these areas are trafficked into the United States each year. Some are recruited within the United States as well.

Human trafficking victims suffer horribly. They live as slaves and are robbed of their humanity. Many never fully recover from the experience. Children are especially vulnerable. Their suffering as trafficking victims begins before their personalities are fully developed. Many suffer from post-traumatic stress disorder (PTSD). People who suffer from PTSD may experience terrible dreams or memories of what

These children, some as young as four years old, did heavy labor in Nigeria. Some had to go through emergency surgeries after they were rescued.

happened to them. They may feel emotionally distant. They may not feel any emotions at all.

There are many other forms of psychological or emotional damage. This damage includes depression, anxiety, phobias, and panic attacks. In addition, child victims of trafficking suffer from shame. Some blame themselves for what happened to them. Some have difficulty trusting others. This makes it hard for them to have healthy relationships. Sometimes it is hard for them to make friends. In some cases, it was their own aunts, uncles, grandparents, or even parents who sold them to traffickers. In other cases, traffickers pretended to be relatives in order to win their trust or to demand their obedience. When trust has been abused, it can be difficult for these victims to learn to trust others again.

Child and adult victims of human trafficking sometimes suffer from what is known as Stockholm Syndrome. This term first came into being to describe a type of relationship that sometimes forms between

Victims

Concerning victims of human trafficking, President George W. Bush said:
"Some are killed. Others die spiritual and emotional deaths, convinced after years of abuse that their lives have no worth. This trade in human beings brings suffering to the innocent and shame to our country, and we will lead the fight against it."[1]

These African boys were kidnapped in Nigeria. They are now forced to dig the soil looking for granite.

kidnapping victims and their captors. Victims are denied contact with the outside world and with other people. As a result, these victims depend on their captors. They can even become sympathetic to their captors. They come to have gratitude for their food, their continued survival, and whatever small privileges they are able to enjoy. When they become free once again, they find it difficult to form normal relationships with others. Often they need the help of counselors to resolve this problem.

There are more problems than the emotional and mental ones. Child victims of human trafficking often suffer from poor physical health as well. Their traffickers or captors save money by feeding them poorly. As a result, many suffer from malnutrition. They also have to work long hours. Many often perform physically demanding work. In many cases, they do not get enough sleep.

At an Indian stone crusher, these children carry heavy stones on their heads.

Many people travel to new countries in hope of a better life. These Chinese girls were caught trying to enter Taiwan.

Their captors provide medical care only when absolutely necessary. By the time the victims are adults, they may have poorly developed muscles and skeletal systems. This can be seen in their poor posture. Their height and weight might be lower than normal for their age. Malnutrition and lack of dental care leaves them with unhealthy teeth and gums. Sometimes they suffer from organ damage as well. For children trafficked into the sex trade, this often means damage to reproductive organs. In many cases, victims of this type of trafficking suffer from unwanted pregnancies or abortions performed against their will. These abortions are often performed under very unclean conditions. The abortions are not always performed by a doctor. They can damage the victim's reproductive systems. They also might contract sexually transmitted infections, hepatitis, and HIV or AIDS. These and other conditions are clues to the possibility that a person might be the victim of trafficking. Law enforcement, immigration, and health-care workers look for these signs.

Child victims of human trafficking have many problems to overcome once they regain their freedom. In addition to their mental, emotional, and medical problems, they also must struggle to readjust to everyday life. If they were enslaved for a long period of time, their entire childhood might have passed

A Growing Trend

"Human trafficking is a low-risk, high-profit enterprise, and because it looks to the casual observer—and even to cops—like garden variety prostitution, it is tolerated. And worse, it is growing."[2]

—Kim Kennedy, CBS Early Show producer

These two teenage girls are working in the red-light district in Calcutta, India. Although India has pledged to protect children from prostitution, other issues often get more attention.

by. They may be adults by the time they are rescued. But they were never allowed to develop normally. Once enslaved, they could no longer live normally as children. Now they find they must live as adults. Typically, these children have little formal education. They lack reading and arithmetic skills as well as other knowledge they would have learned as students. They are also unaware of world events that occurred while they were captives.

Trafficking victims often come from parts of the world where there is much political conflict or economic uncertainty. They sometimes find that their villages or towns have been destroyed. In some cases, their families have become refugees. Or their loved ones also may have become the victims of human traffickers. Worse, loved ones may have been killed. All of these problems make it difficult for victims of human trafficking to adjust to everyday life. It is especially difficult for child victims.

Safe at School?

The U.S. Department of Education reported that school-age children are especially vulnerable to trafficking for sexual exploitation. It says the average age to enter prostitution is between 12 and 14 years old. These children are not always kidnapped. Some traffickers recruit children at school or in after-school programs.

Chapter 5

FREEING ENSLAVED HUMANS

For thousands of years, the human race has sought freedom in many ways. Societies have struggled to gain freedom from the oppression of tyrannical governments. Groups of people have resisted the attempts that others make to overtake them. Individuals have worked to learn about the world. Humans have also challenged the idea that they are doomed to their fates. They learned that they could direct their own futures. These struggles have occurred all over the world. People fought and sacrificed to end slavery. People fought to end rule by conquerors and colonial powers. What can we do to help win the fight for freedom? How can we combat the problem of human trafficking? One way is to make sure people are aware it exists.

In the mid-1990s, two *Baltimore Sun* reporters discussed human trafficking. Gilbert Lewthwaite

This protester rallies at the World Social Forum in Nairobi in 2007. The Forum was first held in Brazil in 2001.

and Gregory Kane had been doing research for a news series about modern-day slavery. At first, their editor was doubtful about what they would be able to find. The pair went to Sudan. There, they were able to do

Treatment

"I was taken by a slave master [who] beat me and shamed me, telling me that I was like a dog."[1]

—*Former Sudanese slave freed by a U.S. church group*

more than just learn about slavery. They were able to purchase and free two Sudanese boys. They paid just $500 for each boy. The boys they freed had been taken from their village and away from their parents. They had been taken in a raid by government forces. For the next six years, they worked on a cattle ranch. They received no pay and had no contact with their families.

Capture

"I was at the market in Abin Dau with my family, including our five children, when the raiders came. We were all taken captive. I was tied by my wrists in a chain to other captives."[2]

—*Report of freed slave in Sudan*

A church group from the United States traveled to Sudan in 1999. Their goal was to win freedom for Christian citizens of that country. These citizens had been enslaved under the National Islamic Front. That government had come to power ten years earlier. The slave traders were asking $100 for each slave. This group was able to free 671 enslaved humans in a single trip to Sudan.

Sudan is just one African nation where slaves are found today.

Stop the Traffik is one group that is committed to ending the problem of modern-day slavery. The group has more than 1,000 member organizations in more than 50 countries. The group raises support and wears symbols of the campaign. They even seek to adapt their own lifestyles so that they are not passively supporting the products of human trafficking. For example, the Stop the Traffik Web site features a challenge. Much of the world's chocolate comes from cocoa beans grown in the Ivory Coast (Cote d'Ivoire). It is likely

Singer Ricky Martin has joined with the United Nations and an activist group called Stop the Traffik to raise awareness and gain support for ending human trafficking.

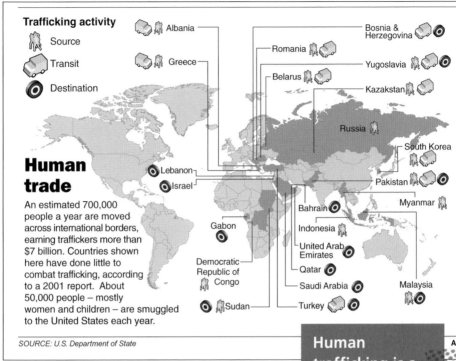

Trafficking activity

Source

Transit

Destination

Human trade

An estimated 700,000 people a year are moved across international borders, earning traffickers more than $7 billion. Countries shown here have done little to combat trafficking, according to a 2001 report. About 50,000 people – mostly women and children – are smuggled to the United States each year.

Albania

Greece

Romania

Belarus

Bosnia & Herzegovina

Yugoslavia

Kazakstan

Russia

South Korea

Pakistan

Myanmar

Lebanon

Israel

Bahrain

Gabon

Indonesia

United Arab Emirates

Qatar

Saudi Arabia

Malaysia

Democratic Republic of Congo

Sudan

Turkey

SOURCE: U.S. Department of State

Human trafficking is a problem that affects all areas of the world.

AP

that children are working on the farms growing the beans. Stop the Traffik is committed to only purchasing child-labor-free chocolate.

Individuals and even groups of individuals cannot succeed alone. The problems of human trafficking and modern-day slavery are widespread. The solution must come from nations acting together. We can give state and local agencies the information they need to identify the victims of human trafficking. We can also give them the tools they need to assist these victims. These tools might include aid to help victims become readjusted to life outside of slavery. Counseling or medical help might be necessary.

The goal is to help government organizations prosecute traffickers and others involved in the trade. The United Nations can impose economic penalties on countries that do not agree with standards in the fight against human trafficking. And we can work within the international community to put pressure on those same nations.

As individuals, we can support leaders who work for this cause. We can also educate others and ourselves about this global problem. Within our own communities, we can avoid supporting businesses we think might be benefiting from human trafficking. We can alert authorities when we believe we have encountered someone participating in or affected by the illegal trade in human beings.

Punishment for Traffickers

"The cooperative efforts of federal agencies and law-enforcement officials will help provide victims the tools and services needed to punish traffickers to the fullest extent of the law."[3]
—*Former U.S. Attorney General John Ashcroft*

Although the Thirteenth Amendment made slavery illegal in the United States, slavery is still occurring. By joining with other nations, we can work together to make slavery and human trafficking a thing of the past.

An Indian woman holds up a sign to remember victims of human trafficking. Organizations that fight against human trafficking remind the world to be aware of human rights abuses occurring today.

Glossary

Anonymous
Unknown or not identified by name.

Captor
A person who confines or imprisons another.

Coercion
The use of force or threats to persuade another to do something.

Consent
Permission or agreement.

Fraud
To trick, deceive, or pretend to be someone you are not.

Labor-intensive
Something that requires a large amount of human input for production.

Malnutrition
A condition caused by a lack of proper or sufficient nutrients in a diet.

Modernization
The process of making something current and up-to-date.

Narcotics
A drug prescribed by a doctor that can be used to dull pain.

Post-Traumatic Stress Disorder
A psychological reaction usually occurring after a stressful event. Symptoms include depression, nervousness, and not being able to sleep.

Prostitute
A person who has sex in exchange for money.

Trafficking
The transportation of goods or people for the purpose of selling and trading.

Transnational
Across national borders.

More Information

Books

Levitin, Sonia. *Dream Freedom*. Orlando, FL: Harcourt, 2000.

Lewis, Barbara A. *The Teen Guide to Global Action: How to Connect With Others (Near & Far) to Create Social Change*. Minneapolis, MN: Free Spirit Publishing, 2007.

Newman, Shirlee P. *Child Slavery in Modern Times*. New York: Franklin Watts, 2000.

Springer, Jane. *Listen to Us: The World's Working Children*. Toronto, ON: Groundwood Books, 1997.

Web Sites

Anti-Slavery International (www.antislavery.org). Anti-Slavery International was founded in 1839. The group concentrates on making slavery a high-priority issue among governments and human rights groups.

Not for Sale Campaign (www.notforsalecampaign.org). The Not for Sale Campaign has started an international abolitionist movement to stop the sale of human beings.

Stop the Traffik (www.stopthetraffik.org). Stop the Traffik seeks to stop the sale of people around the world. The group focuses on advocacy, education, and fundraising.

Notes

Chapter 1. What Is Human Trafficking?

1. Arthur Jones. "Global Slave Trade Prospers." *National Catholic Reporter*. 25 May 2001. 15 May 2008 <http://www.natcath.com/NCR_Online/archives/052501/052501a.htm>.
2. George W. Bush. Address. Tampa, FL. 16 July 2004. 15 May 2008 <http://www.whitehouse.gov/news/releases/2004/07/20040716-11.html>.

Chapter 2. The Demand for Cheap Labor

1. Arthur Jones. "Global Slave Trade Prospers." *National Catholic Reporter*. 25 May 2001. 15 May 2008 <http://www.natcath.com/NCR_Online/archives/052501/052501a.htm>.
2. Beijing Newsroom. "Chinese children sold 'like cabbages' into slavery." *Thomson Reuters*. 29 Apr. 2008. 3 June 2008 <http://www.reuters.com/article/worldNews/idUSPEK27749620080429?feedType=RSS&feedName=worldNews&rpc=22&sp=true>.
3. Associated Press. "Florida a leader in modern slavery." *St. Petersburg Times*. 25 Feb. 2004. 4 June 2008 < http://www.sptimes.com/2004/02/25/State/Florida_a_leader_in_m.shtml>.
4. "Ex-teacher gets 7 years for enslaving Haitian teen." *CNN.com*. 20 May 2008. 1 June 2008 <http://www.cnn.com/2008/CRIME/05/20/woman.enslaved.ap/>.

Chapter 3. Soldiers and the Sex Trade

1. "Definitions." *U.S. Department of State.* 1 June 2008 <http://www.state.gov/g/tip/c16507.htm>.
2. Emily Kaiser. "Sex Trafficking hits home." *Minnesota Daily.* 31 Oct. 2005. 1 June 2008 <http://www.mndaily.com/articles/2005/10/31/65875?print>.
3. "The Realities of Human Trafficking." *CBS News.* 12 Sept. 2007. 1 June 2008 <http://www.cbsnews.com/stories/2007/09/11/earlyshow/main3250963.shtml>.
4. Kim Gamel. "Iraqi Army: 6 Teens Trained as Suicide Bombers." *ABC News.* 26 May 2008. 1 June 2008 <http://abcnews.go.com/International/wireStory?id=4930185>.

Chapter 4. Child Victims of Human Trafficking

1. George W. Bush. Address. Tampa, FL. 16 July 2004. 15 May 2008 <http://www.whitehouse.gov/news/releases/2004/07/20040716-11.html>.
2. "The Realities of Human Trafficking." *CBS News.* 12 Sept. 2007. 1 June 2008 <http://www.cbsnews.com/stories/2007/09/11/earlyshow/main3250963.shtml>.

Chapter 5. Freeing Enslaved Humans

1. "Baroness Caroline Cox: The Price of a Slave." *Christianity Today*. 8 Feb. 1999. 2 June 2008 <http://www.ctlibrary.com/ct/1999/february8/9t2068.html>.
2. Ibid.
3. Catherine Edwards. "Sex-Trade Slave Is Thriving." *BNET*. <http://findarticles.com/p/articles/mi_m1571/is_30_17/ai_77356317>.

Index

About the Author

Thom Winckelmann is a freelance editor, writer, and writing consultant living in Central Florida, where he also teaches college humanities and history. Currently at work on his doctoral dissertation toward a Ph.D. in history, he specializes in Holocaust and genocide studies.

Photo Credits